The ESSENTIALS of

MW01063299

COST & MANAGERIAL ACCOUNTING I

William D. Keller, Ph.D.
Professor of Accounting
Ferris State University, Big Rapids, Michigan

> This book covers the usual course outline of Cost
> & Managerial Accounting I. For additional
> topics, see *"THE ESSENTIALS OF COST &
> MANAGERIAL ACCOUNTING II."*

Research & Education Association
61 Ethel Road West
Piscataway, New Jersey 08854

THE ESSENTIALS ®
OF COST & MANAGERIAL ACCOUNTING I

Printed in the United States of America

Library of Congress Catalog Card Number 97-75935

International Standard Book Number 0-87891-664-4

ESSENTIALS is a registered trademark of
Research & Education Association, Piscataway, New Jersey 08854

WHAT "THE ESSENTIALS" WILL DO FOR YOU

This book is a review and study guide. It is comprehensive and it is concise.

It helps in preparing for exams, in doing homework, and remains a handy reference source at all times.

It condenses the vast amount of detail characteristic of the subject matter and summarizes the **essentials** of the field.

It will thus save hours of study and preparation time.

The book provides quick access to the important facts, principles, theorems, concepts, and equations in the field.

Materials needed for exams can be reviewed in summary form – eliminating the need to read and re-read many pages of textbook and class notes. The summaries will even tend to bring detail to mind that had been previously read or noted.

This "ESSENTIALS" book has been prepared by an expert in the field, and has been carefully reviewed to assure accuracy and maximum usefulness.

Dr. Max Fogiel
Program Director

CONTENTS

Chapter No.		Page No.

1 THE NATURE AND USEFULNESS OF COST ACCOUNTING AND THE ACCOUNTANT'S ROLE — 1

1.1 Definition of Cost Accounting — 1
1.2 Comparison of Cost Accounting with Financial Accounting — 1
1.3 Comparison of CPA Certificate with CMA Certificate — 2
1.4 Comparison of the Offices of Controller and Treasurer — 2
1.5 Costs and Benefits of Accounting — 3
1.6 Line vs. Staff Authority — 4

2 INTRODUCTION TO COST ITEMS AND PURPOSES — 8

2.1 Manufacturing Costs and Merchandising Costs — 8
2.2 Direct and Indirect Labor — 9
2.3 Idle Time — 9
2.4 Overtime Premium — 9
2.5 Labor Fringe Benefits — 10
2.6 Variable and Fixed Costs, and Semi-Variable Costs — 10
2.7 Direct and Indirect Costs — 14
2.8 Controllable and Noncontrollable Costs — 15
2.9 Differential or Incremental Costs — 15
2.10 Opportunity Costs — 16
2.11 Sunk Costs — 17

3	**ACCOUNTING FOR COST FLOWS AND ACCUMULATION. COST BEHAVIOR.**	**21**
3.1	Cost Flows of a Mercantile Business	21
3.2	Cost Flows of a Manufacturing Business	22
3.3	Perpetual vs. Periodic Inventories	25
3.4	Actual Costs vs. Applied Costs. The Factory Overhead Control Account	26
3.5	Underapplied vs. Overapplied Factory Overhead	27
3.6	Cost Accumulation	28
3.7	Cost Behavior	28
4	**COST-VOLUME-PROFIT RELATIONSHIPS**	**32**
4.1	Contribution Margin, and Contribution Margin Ratio	32
4.2	Break-Even Point	33
4.3	Target Profits	
4.4	Margin of Safety	35
4.5	Profit Maximization	36
4.6	The Profit Equation	37
4.7	Income Taxes	37
4.8	Finding Targeted Sales Dollars	38
4.9	Cost-Profit-Volume Analysis with Semi-Fixed Costs	39
4.10	Multi-Product Cost-Profit-Volume Analysis	40
4.11	Sensitivity Analysis	40
4.12	Predatory Pricing	40
4.13	Irrelevance of Past (Sunk) Costs	40
4.14	Capacity Costs	41
4.15	Curvilinear Variable Costs	41
4.16	Learning Curve	41
4.17	Discretionary Costs	41
5	**PRODUCT COSTING METHODS**	**45**
5.1	Variable Costing vs. Full AbsorptionCosting	45
5.2	Overhead Application Rates	45

5.3	Actual, Normal, or Standard Costing	47

6	**JOB ORDER COSTING**	**49**
6.1	Job Order vs. Process Costing	49
6.2	Source Documents of Job Costing	49
6.3	Cost Flows for Job Order Costing	49
6.4	Direct and Indirect Materials	50
6.5	Accounting for Labor in Job Order Cost Accounting	50
6.6	Accounting for Manufacturing Overhead in Job Order Cost Accounting	51
6.7	Transfers to Finished Goods in Job Order Cost Accounting	51
6.8	Transfers to Cost of Goods Sold in Job Order Cost Accounting	52
6.9	Applying Factory Overhead	52
6.10	Two Ways of Closing Out Factory Overhead Control	54
6.11	Computation of Spending Variances	56
6.12	Computation of Production Volume Variances	56
6.13	Job Cost Sheets	57
6.14	Stores Requisitions	58
6.15	Work Tickets	58
6.16	Clock Cards	59
6.17	Responsibility Centers	59

7	**PROCESS COSTING**	**64**
7.1	What Process Costing Does	64
7.2	Equivalent Units	64
7.3	Assigning Costs to Units	64
7.4	Incomplete Units In Beginning And Ending Inventories (First-In, First-Out)	64
7.5	Production Cost Report	66
7.6	Spoilage Computations	66
7.7	Sequential Processing	67
7.8	Parallel Processing	67
7.9	Flow of Materials, Labor and Overhead Costs in Process Costing	67

8. **COST ALLOCATION IN SERVICE DEPARTMENTS AND SEGMENTED REPORTING** 69

8.1 The Nature of Service Departments 69
8.2 Direct Method of Allocation of Costs 69
8.3 The Step Method of Allocation of Costs 69
8.4 The Reciprocal Method 70
8.5 Plantwide vs. Department Rates 70
8.6 Engineered Costs, Discretionary Costs, and Committed Costs 70
8.7 Operating Leverage 71

9 **VARIABLE COSTING** 74

9.1 Difference Between Variable and Full (Absorption) Costing 74
9.2 Advantages of Variable Costing 75
9.3 Advantages of Absorption Costing 76

10 **MASTER BUDGETS AND STANDARDS** 78

10.1 Purpose of Budgets 78
10.2 Time Coverage of Budgets 78
10.3 Pro Forma Statements 78
10.4 Operation Budget 78
10.5 Financial Budget 79
10.6 Sales Budget 79
10.7 Production Budget 79
10.8 Direct Labor Budget 80
10.9 Cost of Goods Sold Budget 80
10.10 Cash Budget 81
10.11 Participative Budgeting 81
10.12 The Delphi Technique (To help forecasting and reduce bias) 81

11 **FLEXIBLE BUDGETS** 84

11.1 Flexible Budgets 84
11.2 Continuous (Perpetual) Budgets 86
11.3 Participative (Self Imposed) Budgets 86
11.4 Sales Forecasting 86
11.5 Just-In-Time Inventory Systems 87
11.6 Zero-Base Budgeting (In-Depth Review) 88

CHAPTER 1

THE NATURE AND USEFULNESS OF COST ACCOUNTING AND THE ACCOUNTANT'S ROLE

1.1 DEFINITION OF COST ACCOUNTING

Cost Accounting–A sub-field of accounting that records, measures, and reports information about costs. A cost is a sacrifice of resources. Cost Accounting is Management Accounting (Internal Accounting) plus some external reporting.

Management Accounting–(Internal Accounting)–The identification, measurement, accumulation, analysis, preparation, interpretation, and communication of information that assists executives in fulfilling objectives of their organization.

1.2 COMPARISON OF COST ACCOUNTING WITH FINANCIAL ACCOUNTING

Cost Accounting:

1. Looks to the future
2. Subjective
3. Reports mainly for internal consumption
4. Mainly to cut costs and expenses

Financial Accounting:

1. Looks to the past
2. Objective
3. Reports mainly for external consumption
4. Covers the whole field

1

1.3 COMPARISON OF CPA CERTIFICATE WITH CMA CERTIFICATE

Certified Public Accountant:	Certified Management Accountant:
1. Exam written by American Institute of Certified Public Accountants	1. Exam written by National Association of Accountants
2. Exam given in November and May	2. Exam given in December and June
3. Exam consists of four parts	3. Exam consists of five parts
4. Must be college graduate with major in accounting	4. Must be college graduate with major in business
5. Covers accounting theory and practice, auditing, and business law	5. Covers all aspects of business, focusing on decision making
6. Requires usually two years of work in a public accounting office with employer's written recommendation	6. Experience requirements are subject to change.

1.4 COMPARISON OF THE OFFICES OF CONTROLLER AND TREASURER

Controller:	Treasurer:
1. Chief Accountant of the Corporation	1. Chief financial officer of the corporation
2. Accounting for special reports, planning & control, internal audits	2. Managing cash
3. Tax accounting and Planning	3. Obtaining investment capital

4. Cost records and Property accounting
5. Government Reporting
6. Protection of Assets
7. Economic Appraisal

4. Banking
5. Insurance
6. Investor Relations

1.5 COSTS AND BENEFITS OF ACCOUNTING

How much accounting for managerial purposes is enough?

Are the benefits derived from managerial cost accounting high enough to exceed the expenses?

Should a computerized inventory system be installed?

a. Costs and Benefits of accounting are difficult to measure.

b. Users can see the benefits of accounting information supplied them, but accountants are most familiar with the costs.

The Value of Information – Accurate analysis of information.

The company is trying to decide whether or not to accept a one-time order. If the order is accepted, the increased revenue to the company will be $1,000,000. The costs of making the product for the special order are not known with certainty, but they are estimated to be either $800,000 or $1,200,000, depending on how much time is needed for its manufacture. So, acceptance of the order would result in a net gain of $200,000 or a net loss of $200,000, whereas rejection will produce neither gain nor loss.

3

The owner regards the two production cost events as having the following probabilities: (1) There is a .7 probability that production costs will be $800,000, so there would be a $200,000 profit; (2) There is a .3 probability that production costs will be $1,200,000, hence a $200,000 loss if the order is accepted.

EV = the expected value of the outcomes
PR_I = the probability of each outcome occurring
V_I = the value of each outcome

$EV = \Sigma\, PR_I\, V_I\,; = (.7 \times \$200,000) + (.3 \times -\$200,000) = +\$80,000$

Thus, since the probability that production costs will only be $800,000 is 70%, there is a probability for an $80,000 profit in accepting the one-time order.

1.6   LINE vs. STAFF AUTHORITY

Line–People who perform a line function are responsible for supervision, guidance, and decision making. There is a chain of command from the president to upper-, middle-, and lower-level managers.

Staff–People who perform a staff function provide advice and service to other members in the organization but cannot require implementation of their recommendations. Staff members have no authority over the line personnel but provide specialized help to the various departments. (Example: Company nurse)

Line and staff managers within the corporate organization should be clearly defined on organization charts.

REVIEW QUESTIONS

1. How do costs differ from expenses?

Costs usually have to do with the value of merchandise purchased in a mercantile business or the value of the goods manufactured in a manufacturing firm. They are usually placed in the top portion of the income statement as part of the computation of cost of goods sold and are part of the computation of gross income. Expenses are listed toward the bottom of the income statement after gross profit – below the gross profit line – and usually consist of selling expenses and office expenses. They are to be found in both manufacturing and mercantile firms.

2. Is cost accounting the same as management accounting?

Most authorities consider these the same, but some authorities believe that management accounting is somewhat broader than cost accounting. These authorities believe that cost accounting is completely within the business while management accounting could also include some reporting outside the business.

3. Is beginning accounting usually considered cost accounting or financial accounting?

Financial accounting.

4. How does cost accounting differ from financial accounting?

Cost accounting reports to higher-ups within the firm while financial accounting stresses mainly outside reports. Cost accounting's main thrust is to cut costs while financial accounting stresses revenue, costs, and expenses. Cost accounting exists chiefly to implement future plans while financial accounting is to summarize figures for the year just past.

5. What are the educational requirements for the CPA Certificate?

College graduate from accredited college with accounting major.

6. What are the experience requirements for the CPA Certificate?

In most states, two years of successful work in a CPA office.

7. What are the testing requirements for the CPA certificate?

Pass a national test of four parts, given in November and May. These four parts are: Auditing, Business Law, Accounting Theory and Accounting Practice.

8. What can a CPA do that a public accountant without a CPA cannot do?

Use the "attest function" at the end of an audit, stating "These books follow generally accepted accounting and auditing principles and practice." Also CPA's can audit government books.

9. Do CPA's have state licensure?

Yes.

10. What are the experience requirements for the CMA Certificate?

Certified Management Accountants need two years of successful management experience, but these requirements are subject to change.

11. What are the education requirements for the CMA Certificate?

Four years of college with a business major – requirements subject to change.

12. What are the testing requirements for the CMA Certificate?

Must pass an exam put out by the National Association of Accountants covering broad fields of management and economics.

13. Do CMA's have state licensure?

No.

14. How do the offices of controller and treasurer for a corporation differ?

Controller is chief accountant and treasurer is chief financial officer. Controller is in charge of economic appraisal, protection of assets, government reporting, cost records, and tax accounting and planning. Treasurer is in charge of money handling and management, investor problems, banking and insurance.

15. How much managerial accounting should a firm have?

Cost-benefit approach. No more money should be spent on management accounting than the financial benefits to be derived. These are often difficult to determine.

16. Should a company have line authority, staff authority, or both?

This depends on the size of the company, its purpose, and the products it sells and manufactures. With the complicated business system of today, most large corporations have both line and staff authority.

CHAPTER 2

INTRODUCTION TO COST TERMS AND PURPOSES

2.1 MANUFACTURING COSTS AND MERCHANDISING COSTS

A manufacturing firm is more complex than a merchandising firm. Manufacturing involves changing raw materials into finished products. So a manufacturing firm is involved in production as well as in marketing and administration. Cost of a manufactured product is made up of:

Direct Materials–Raw materials that actually go into the product.

Direct Labor–People's salaries on the production line.

Manufacturing Overhead–All other factory costs (rent, heat, light, depreciation of factory equipment, factory property taxes, insurance).

Non-Manufacturing Costs:

Marketing (selling) Costs–Order-getting and order-filling costs (salesmen's salaries, salesmen's travel, transportation out).

Administrative Costs–Office salaries, officers' salaries, depreciation of office machines and furniture, taxes on office building.

Product Costs–Direct materials, direct labor, factory overhead.

Period Costs–Selling and administrative costs.

A Mercantile Business, such as a hardware store, has period costs (selling and administrative costs), but since it doesn't manufacture any goods, it has no product costs.

A Broom Factory, since it manufactures and sells brooms, has both product and period costs.

2.2 DIRECT AND INDIRECT LABOR

Direct laborers work directly on the production line and are actually involved in the manufacture of the products.

Indirect laborers work in the factory but not directly on the production line – janitors, factory machine repairers, lawn workers. (Indirect labor for cost accounting purposes is part of Manufacturing Overhead).

2.3 IDLE TIME

The costs of direct labor workers who are unable to perform their work due to machine breakdowns, materials shortages, power failure, etc. These are treated in cost accounting as manufacturing overhead, not as direct labor cost.

2.4 OVERTIME PREMIUM

Extra pay for work over 8 hours per day or over 40 hours per

9

week, or for Saturday or Sunday or other holiday work. This is part of manufacturing overhead.

Direct labor ($15 x 44 hours)	$660
Manufacturing Overhead (overtime premium: $7.50 x 4 hours)	30
Total cost for the week	$690

2.5 LABOR FRINGE BENEFITS

Employer-related costs paid by the employer–health insurance, life insurance, retirement plans, hospitalization plans, vacation pay.

Some firms charge fringe benefits to manufacturing overhead, and some charge these to direct labor. (Charging fringe benefits of direct laborers to Direct Labor is preferred.)

2.6 VARIABLE AND FIXED COSTS, AND SEMI-VARIABLE COSTS

Variable Costs change, in total, in direct proportion to changes in the level of activity. (Examples: Direct materials and direct labor.) If the output of brooms in the broom factory doubles the second month in comparison to the first month, the total amount spent on direct materials or direct labor should also double. Cost of material per unit or pay per hour should remain the same however.

Fixed Costs remain the same in total, regardless of changes in activity level. (Example: Monthly rent on the factory. Let us say its $100 per month. Even if the output of broom production doubles the second month as compared to the first month, the monthly rent payment should remain at $100 per month. Although the total rent payment per month remains the same, the "rent per unit of output" would fluctuate.)

Semi-Variable Costs (also called mixed costs) have some features like variable costs and some like fixed costs. (Example: Electricity customers may have a monthly minimum bill no matter how little electricity they use. This would be the fixed element. The amount used over the fixed minimum would be the variable element.)

Example in graph form as to the way variable costs work: First the table, then the graph which explains the table.

VARIABLE COSTS

Number of Trucks Produced	Radiator Cost Per Truck	Total Radiator Cost
100	$30	$ 3,000
200	$30	$ 6,000
300	$30	$ 9,000
400	$30	$12,000
500	$30	$15,000
600	$30	$18,000

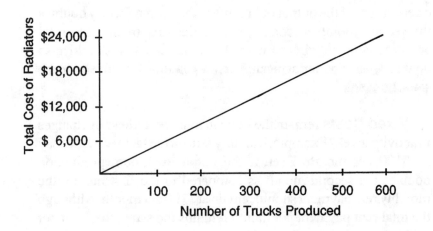

11

As the number of trucks produced increases, the total dollar value of the radiators increases proportionately, as shown in the diagonal line, although the radiator cost per truck remains the same – $30.

FIXED COSTS

Number of Trucks Produced	Rent of Factory	Rent per Unit Produced
100	$100 per month	$1 rent per truck
200	$100 per month	$.50 rent per truck
300	$100 per month	$.333 rent per truck
400	$100 per month	$.25 rent per truck
500	$100 per month	$.20 rent per truck
600	$100 per month	$.167 rent per truck

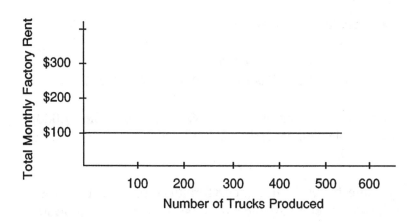

Even though the number of trucks produced increases each month, the amount of total factory rent remains at $100 per month, as shown in the parallel line at $100. However, (as column 3 in the table on the previous page shows), as the number of trucks produced each month increases, the rent per truck decreases. (Rent per truck = total factory rent divided by number of trucks produced).

Semi-Variable Costs—(Mixed Costs) have both fixed and variable elements. Let us say that the corporation's agreement with the electric company is to pay a minimum of $1,000 per month for its outside lights which are turned on every night whether the factory is operating or not. Let us also say that the variable element is $.20 more per kilowatt-hour used.

Let X = fixed cost element (In this case, $1,000)
Let Y = variable rate (In this case, $.20)
Let the number in the formula = the number of kilowatt hours actually used.

Let us say in the first month there were 10,000 kilowatt hours of electricity actually used.

The formula would then be:

$$X + \$.20Y =$$
$$\$1,000 + \$.20 (10,000) = \$1,000 + \$2,000 = \$3,000$$

Thus, the fixed element of the semi-variable cost is the $1,000, and the variable element is the $2,000, or the total semi-variable cost is $3,000.

Carrying the semi-variable cost formula further, the following table shows the semi-variable cost for several levels of kilowatt-hour output:

$$X + \$.20Y =$$
$$\$1,000 + \$.20 (10,000) = \$1,000 + \$2,000 = \$\ 3,000$$
$$\$1,000 + \$.20 (20,000) = \$1,000 + \$4,000 = \$\ 5,000$$

13

$1,000 +$.20 (30,000) = $1,000 + $ 6,000 = $ 7,000
$1,000 +$.20 (40,000) = $1,000 + $ 8,000 = $ 9,000
$1,000 +$.20 (50,000) = $1,000 + $10,000 = $11,000

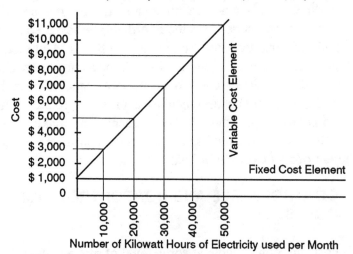

Number of Kilowatt Hours of Electricity used per Month

The horizontal line at the $1,000 level is the fixed-cost element in the semi-variable costs.

The diagonal line beginning at the left margin at the $1,000 level shows the variable cost element.

For the first line of the table, at the 10,000 kilowatt level, the total cost is $3,000, of which $1,000 is fixed cost and the remaining $2,000 is variable cost.

For the bottom line of the table, at the 50,000 kilowatt level, the total cost is $11,000, of which $1,000 is fixed cost and the remaining $10,000 is variable cost.

2.7   DIRECT AND INDIRECT COSTS

A direct cost can be physically traced to a product line, a sales territory, a division, or some other sub-part of the company. If the

14

segment under consideration is a product line, then the materials and labor would both be direct costs.

An indirect cost cannot be physically traced to a specific product line, so it must be allocated in order to be assigned to the segment under consideration. An example of this is Manufacturing Overhead. These are general, overall operating activities. They are called indirect costs or common costs. It must be allocated in order to be assigned to a unit of product. This allocation is arbitrary, although the company may make guidelines, such as relative floor space in each department for the assignment of rent expense or heat expense.

2.8 CONTROLLABLE AND NONCONTROLLABLE COSTS

All costs are controllable at some level of management.

Only at the lower levels of management can some costs be considered non-controllable – such things as hiring and firing, expanding and contracting facilities, and setting expenditure policies. The only controllable costs at the lower levels of management are those that the lower manager is **authorized to control**. For instance, the length of the coffee break for line employees, or the amount of entertainment expense for salesmen.

Non-Controllable Costs for lower level managers might be rent expense or depreciation expense.

2.9 DIFFERENTIAL OR INCREMENTAL COSTS

In making management decisions (like "make-or-buy" decisions) managers compare alternatives. Any cost that is present under one alternative is known as a differential cost (incremental cost). (An economist calls this "marginal cost.")

15

2. Differential Costs can be either fixed or variable.

3. Example: Let us assume that the Fuller Brush Company is thinking about changing its marketing method from direct door-to-door sales to distribution through retailers. Present costs and revenues are compared to projected costs and revenues as follows:

V = Variable; F = Fixed

	Direct Door-to-Door Sales (Present)	Retailer Distribution (Proposed)	Differential Costs and Revenues
Revenues (V)	$800,000	$900,000	$100,000
Cost of Goods Sold (V)	$300,000	$350,000	$ 50,000
Advertising (F)	$ 30,000	$ 50,000	$ 20,000
Commissions (V)	$ 50,000	0	$ (50,000)
Warehouse Depreciation (F)	$ 40,000	$ 30,000	$ (10,000)
Other Expenses (F)	$ 60,000	$ 60,000	0
Total Expenses	$480,000	$490,000	$ 10,000
Net Income	$320,000	$410,000	$ 90,000

Looking at the extreme right-hand column of the table, the differential revenue of $100,000 less the differential expenses of $10,000 leaves a differential net income of $90,000, so it would be valuable, in this case, for Fuller Brush Company to switch to the proposed Retailer Distribution Method.

2.10 OPPORTUNITY COSTS

Opportunity Costs–potential benefits that are lost when the choice of one course of action makes it necessary to give up

16

a competing course of action.

Example: A firm is considering investing $10,000 in land to be held for building a warehouse in the future. At present this $10,000 is invested in a government bond at 7% earning $700 per year interest. If the firm cashes in the bond and buys the land, the $700 per year interest income would be given up, so this is an **Opportunity Cost**. (They lose $700 now, but have the opportunity to build on their own property at a later date.)

2.11 SUNK COSTS

Sunk Costs–Costs that have already been incurred and that cannot be changed by any decision made now or in the future. (They are not differential costs, because present decisions cannot help with sunk costs.)

Example: Let us say we have already bought a factory machine for $20,000. Soon we realize that this was not a good buy and the machine does not fit in with our production needs. The expenditure has already been made. It has been unwise. No future decision can cause the cost to be avoided.

Let us assume that we cannot sell the machine to anyone else.

REVIEW QUESTIONS

1. How does a manufacturing firm differ from a mercantile business?
More complex set of books. Must show manufacturing costs as well as operating expenses. A manufacturing firm manufactures and sells goods, while a mercantile firm only sells goods.

2. What are the three major factory costs?
Direct material, direct labor and manufacturing overhead.

3. Of what does manufacturing overhead consist?

All the other factory costs except direct labor and direct materials. These would include indirect labor such as janitor salaries, indirect material or material not directly used in producing the goods, such as janitor floor-cleaning compound, depreciation on factory machinery, factory building rent, factory utilities.

4. What types of costs are common to both mercantile and factory businesses?

Operating expenses such as salesmen's salaries, delivery expenses, and office salaries.

5. How do product costs differ from period costs?

Product costs add to the value of the product being produced in the factory and consist of direct materials, direct labor, and factory overhead. Period costs are operating expenses.

6. How does direct labor differ from indirect labor?

Direct labor costs are wages of production-line workers, and indirect labor costs are wages of people who do not work directly on the production line, such as janitors and floor supervisors.

7. What is idle time, and how is it charged on the books?

This is the cost of paying direct laborers for downtime. This cost is usually charged to Factory Overhead, not to Direct Labor.

8. What are labor fringe benefits, and how are they charged on the books?

These are extra costs that modern employers are expected to shoulder because of union contracts. They also keep the employees happier and less inclined to quit and find other work. They include health insurance and vacations and retirement plans.

9. How do fixed costs differ from variable costs? Give examples.

Fixed costs remain the same in total even though production varies from month to month. Example: Rent of factory building.

Variable costs increase or decrease in proportion to the monthly rise or fall of production. Example: Direct labor costs. If production triples in the second month as compared to the first month, then direct labor costs should also triple.

10. What are semi-variable costs?

These are costs that are partly fixed and partly variable. They are also called mixed costs. At a production level, the variable portion should be added to the fixed portion to get the total semi-variable cost at that level. Example: A salesman who has a contract with the firm to get a certain minimum wage per month (Fixed Portion) plus a commission (Variable Portion).

11. How do direct costs differ from indirect costs?

In apportioning total costs to various departments of the firm, a cost that can be directly traced to specific departments is a direct cost. Let us assume that there is an electricity meter in each department, and by merely reading each department's meter each month, we can get the amount of electricity each department has used.

An indirect cost is one that cannot be directly apportioned to the various departments because there is no direct way of determining how much of the total cost should be charged to each. An example would be rent expense. Let us say the total rent for the factory is $500 per month. Let us say there are 5 departments. Should each department be charged $100? Or should the apportionment be by some other method such as sales of each department, or floor space used, or electricity used? No matter which method of apportionment is chosen, it is just a guess, since there is no completely accurate method of apportionment in this case.

12. How does a controllable cost differ from a non-controllable cost, and are these the same as fixed costs?

All costs are controllable at the highest levels of a corporation. Even fixed costs such as rent expense are controllable by the president of the corporation – if rent is raised, he may decide to move to cheaper quarters. Non-Controllable costs are only non-controllable at lower management levels. For instance, a department head may be able to control the length of time for coffee break, but he cannot cut down the depreciation expense on machinery charged to his department.

Controllable and non-controllable costs are not the same as fixed costs.

13. What are differential costs?

In making a decision, like whether or not to accept a special production order, the extra costs to be expended or the costs to be saved in making this choice are compared to the present costs of not making the choice – not taking the order. The difference between these costs is called differential costs. This should be determined before making the decision.

14. What are Opportunity Costs, and why are they important to the cost accountant?

Opportunity costs are the benefits or opportunities given up by making a management decision. For instance, a young man is employed at $15,000 per year. He decides to go back to college and quit his job. He loses $15,000 each year for the opportunity to get a college education.

CHAPTER 3

ACCOUNTING FOR COST FLOWS AND ACCUMULATION. COST BEHAVIOR.

3.1 COST FLOWS OF A MERCANTILE BUSINESS

Merchandising companies purchase goods already manufactured:

No direct Material, or Direct Labor, or Manufacturing Overhead.

No Work in Process Account.

Finished Goods is simply called Merchandise Inventory.

Purchases are debited to Merchandise Inventory.

Measurement of buyer's performance.

Variance: Compare actual costs debited to inventory with budget costs allowed for goods purchased.

Cost of the units sold during the period is transferred to Cost of Goods Sold. (Debit Cost of Goods Sold and credit Merchandise Inventory.)

Marketing and Administrative Expenses are "value added" in merchandising, but they are not added to the value of the inventory.

In a mercantile business a product's cost is generally its purchase price plus the cost of transporting the merchandise.

Example of Cost Flows in a mercantile business:

Merchandise Inventory
    Accounts Payable
        (Buy inventory on account)
Cost of Goods Sold
    Merchandise Inventory
        (Record cost price of inventory sold)
Marketing and Administrative Costs
    Accounts Payable
        (Record salary expense, salesmen's expense, etc.)
Accounts Receivable
    Sales
        (To record sales on account at sales price)

3.2 COST FLOWS OF A MANUFACTURING BUSINESS

Cost Flows through Direct Materials Inventory Account

Direct Materials Inventory	
Beginning Inventory	
+ Materials Purchased	Direct Materials
	Used in Factory————>
Total = Material Available for	
Use in Factory	
Ending Materials Inventory	

Cost Flows through the Work in Process Inventory Account.

Work in Process Inventory

Beginning Work in Process
Inventory
————> +   Direct Materials   Cost Allocated to
              Used in Production   Finished Units————>
       +   Direct Labor
       +   Factory Overhead

Total

Ending Inventory for Work in Process

Cost Flows through the Finished Goods Inventory Account.

Finished Goods Inventory

Beginning Finished Goods
Inventory
————> + Cost of Units Finished   Cost of Units
          This Period   Sold this Period ————>

Total = Finished Units
           Available for Sale

Ending Finished Goods Inventory

Cost Flows into the Cost of Goods Sold Account.

Cost of Goods Sold

——>Cost of Units Sold
    this period

Cost Flows of a Manufacturing Business

Journal Entries

1. Purchase of raw materials on account

Raw Materials Inventory
    Accounts Payable (or Cash)

2. Use of direct materials in the factory

Work in Process Inventory
    Raw Materials Inventory

3. Use of indirect materials in the factory

Factory Overhead Control
    Raw Materials Inventory

4. Use of direct labor in the factory

Work in Process Inventory
    Wages Payable

5. Application of Factory Overhead to Production

Work in Process Inventory
    Factory Overhead Control

6. Movement of completed product from factory to finished goods warehouse

Finished Goods Inventory
    Work in Process Inventory

7a. Movement of sold merchandise from Finished Goods Warehouse to trucks and trains (cost price)

Cost of Goods Sold
    Finished Goods Inventory

7b. Movement of sold merchandise from Finished Goods Warehouse to trucks and trains (sales price)

Accounts Receivable (or Cash)
    Sales

3.3 PERPETUAL vs. PERIODIC INVENTORIES

Perpetual Inventory–Requires a continuous record of additions to and reductions in materials, work in process, and finished goods on a day-to-day basis.

Example of a perpetual inventory card (First-in First-out Method):

Harmon's Vegetable Soup

Date	Purchases	Cost of Sales	Balance
1/1/88	Balance		500 cans @ $1.00 = $500.00
1/2/88	50 cans @ $1.10 = $ 55.00		500 cans @ $1.00 = $500.00 50 cans @ $1.10 = $ 55.00
1/8/88	40 cans @ $1.05 = $ 42.00		500 cans @ $1.00 = $500.00 50 cans @ $1.10 = $ 55.00 40 cans @ $1.05 = $ 42.00
		500 cans @ $1.00 = $500.00 40 cans @ $1.10 = $ 44.00	10 cans @ $1.10 = $ 11.00 40 cans @ $1.05 = $ 42.00

Example of periodic inventory:

Beginning Inventories (by physical count)	$ 88,000	Goods Available	$188,000
Add: Manufacturing Costs (direct materials used, direct labor, factory overhead)	100,000	Less: Ending Inventory (by physical count)	24,000
Cost of Goods Available for Sale	$188,000	Cost of Goods Sold	$164,000

3.4   ACTUAL COSTS vs. APPLIED COSTS. THE FACTORY OVERHEAD CONTROL ACCOUNT

Application Rate

At the beginning of the year the application rate for the year is computed by dividing the Budgeted Overhead by some denominator such as: direct labor hours, direct labor dollars, machine hours, or direct material costs. This denominator (divisor) is chosen by the denominator which "best fits" the rises and falls of the budgeted overhead.

Examples:

$$\frac{\$ 879,500 \text{ Budgeted Overhead}}{50,000 \text{ direct labor hrs. budgeted}} = \$17.59 \text{ per direct labor hour}$$

$$\frac{\$ 879,500 \text{ Budgeted Overhead}}{\$ 500,000 \text{ direct labor cost}} = 1.759, \text{ or } (175.9\%)$$

Estimated Overhead Costs are 175.9% of estimated direct labor costs.

The Factory Overhead Control is a temporary account often closed out into Cost of Goods Sold, but also sometimes closed out into Work in Process Inventory and Finished Goods Inventory, along with Cost of Goods Sold. As bills come in during the month and right after the end of the month, Factory Overhead Control is debited. After all bills are in, we total the debit side of the account. At month's end, or before that, if a shipment of finished goods is leaving the finished goods warehouse, we apply the overhead to production by debiting Work in Process and crediting Factory Overhead Control for the applied figure (guessed amount of the overhead).

26

FACTORY OVERHEAD CONTROL

Actual		Applied
Indirect Materials		
(Supplies)	$505.00	(79 hours worked times
Indirect Labor	300.00	the computed rate per
Utilities of the		direct labor hour $17.59)
factory	600.00	
Depreciation of		
Factory Machinery ...	100.00	
	$1,505.00	$1,389.61

The 79 hours come from the time tickets received by the accounting department from the factory floor. This is multiplied by the predetermined rate ($17.59 per direct labor hour) to give an approximation of the costs before all the month's bills have been received.

3.5 UNDERAPPLIED vs. OVERAPPLIED FACTORY OVERHEAD

FACTORY OVERHEAD CONTROL

Actual		Applied	
			$1,389.61
		(Closing)	115.39
	$1,505.00		$1,505.00

Look closely at the figure on the credit (right) side of the account ($1,389.61). If this applied figure is too low, (lower than the one on the left), it is underapplied. If it is too high, it is overapplied. You will notice that in the case above, it is underapplied by $115.39 (the difference between $1,505.00 and $1,389.61).

At the end of the period this number ($115.39) is closed out, usually into Cost of Goods Sold. But if much of the inventory at period's end is still in the factory or in the finished goods warehouse, the overapplied or underapplied amount could be closed out proportionately into three accounts: Work in Process, Finished Goods, and Cost of Goods Sold.

3.6   COST ACCUMULATION

Cost Accumulation–As the partially finished goods move through the factory, the total value of these goods continues to increase, because more work and overhead are being used on them.

3.7   COST BEHAVIOR

As production increases (or decreases) in the factory month by month, the total variable costs increase proportionately to the increase in production. However, the variable costs per unit remain the same.

As production increases in the factory month by month, the total fixed costs remain the same; however, the fixed costs per unit are proportionately inverse. That is, as production increases the fixed costs per unit decrease. (Or, as production decreases, the fixed costs per unit increase.)

Semi-Variable costs (such as electricity) have some of the behavior of fixed costs and some of the behavior of variable costs. They should be divided into their variable cost component and their fixed cost component before computation.

REVIEW QUESTIONS

1. What is meant by Cost Flow?

The movement of costs from one account to the other as merchandise comes into the business or goes out of the business, or as merchandise goes from one department to another within the business.

2. Why are cost flows simpler in a mercantile business than in a manufacturing business?

A mercantile business merely buys and sells merchandise, not converting it from raw materials to finished products as does a manufacturing business.

3. Are marketing and administrative expenses of the business added to the value of the inventory?

No. They must be considered in pricing the product in order to make a profit, but they are not added into the inventory costs.

4. How are transportation costs handled on the books of a mercantile business?

They are usually added in to the value of the merchandise inventory.

5. Are indirect materials placed in the Work in Process Inventory?

No, they are debited to the Factory Overhead Control account.

6. Work in Process Inventory and the other inventories are considered asset accounts. Would Factory Overhead Control also be an asset account?

No, it is a temporary account and must be closed out into other accounts at the end of the fiscal period.

7. How does the cost flow work in a manufacturing business?

Materials are purchased from a vendor; they are then used in the factory and combined with labor and overhead to produce finished products. The finished products are stored in a warehouse then sold.

8. Since a running record of perpetual inventory is kept daily, does inventory have to be counted at year's end?

Yes, it should be counted to determine losses, if any.

9. Do most businesses use perpetual or periodic inventory systems?

It used to be that larger businesses kept perpetual inventories and smaller businesses used the periodic or physical system of inventory. Now, when most businesses use computers, more and more are switching to the perpetual inventory system.

10. Why are application rates for overhead figured?

Overhead costs must be known at the time the goods leave the finished goods warehouse. Management cannot wait until after the end of the month when all the bills finally come in. So the overhead rate is computed for the whole year at the beginning of the year, and this rate is multiplied by the denominator value – such as hours actually worked on the job – to determine the applied or guessed value.

11. If the overhead is underapplied, is this favorable or unfavorable?

It is unfavorable, because we guessed less than what the overhead actually cost.

12. How does a person know how to close out the Factory Overhead Control account?

Usually it is closed out into Cost of Goods Sold. If the debit side of the Factory Overhead Control Account is higher than the credit side, it will have a debit balance. In this case, close it by debiting Cost of Goods Sold and crediting Factory Overhead Control.

13. Since fixed and variable costs have different behaviors, how can these be stated to show consistency at all levels of production?

Variable costs should be stated at value per unit and fixed costs should be stated at total value.

CHAPTER 4

COST-VOLUME-PROFIT RELATIONSHIPS

4.1 CONTRIBUTION MARGIN, AND CONTRIBUTION MARGIN RATIO

Contribution Margin is net sales less variable costs and expenses.

Contribution Margin can be figured either in total or per unit.

1. Sales per unit $10.00
   Less variable costs per unit.................................. 7.00
   Contribution Margin per unit .... $ 3.00

2. Let us imagine that we sold 100 units at $10 per unit, or (100 units x $10 = $1,000)

   Sales in total.. $1,000.00
   Variable costs ($7 per unit x 100 units) 700.00
   Contribution Margin in total
   ($3 per unit x 100 units)...................................... $ 300.00

Contribution Margin Ratio is computed by dividing the Contribution Margin in dollars by the total sales. (If Contribution Margin is $300 and total sales are $1,000, then divide $300 by

$1,000, getting a Contribution Margin Ratio of 30%. This means that the Contribution Margin, in this case, is 30% of sales.

4.2   BREAK-EVEN POINT

Break-Even Point–The place where total costs and total revenues are equal. The point where a business makes neither profit nor loss. (This computation is useful in planning for future business operations.)

Formula for finding Beak-Even Point in units of product:

$$\text{Break-Even Point in units} = \frac{\text{Fixed Costs per Period}}{\text{Contribution Margin per unit}}$$

Let us imagine that the budgeted fixed costs for next year are $12,000 and the Contribution Margin per unit is $3.

$$\text{4,000 units (Break-Even Point)} = \frac{\$12,000}{\$3}$$

If the fixed costs are $12,000 and the Contribution Margin is $3, we divide $12,000 by $3 and get a Break-Even Point of 4,000 units. Thus, if we sell 4,000 units next year, we make neither profit nor loss.

First formula for finding Break-Even Point in dollars:

a.   Multiply the Break-Even Point in units by the sales price per unit.

b.   Example: 4,000 units sold at Break-Even Point times $10 sales per unit = $40,000, the Break-Even Point in dollars.

Second formula for finding Break-Even Point in dollars:

$$\text{Break-Even Point in Dollars} = \frac{\text{Fixed Costs per Period}}{\text{Contribution Margin Ratio}}$$

$$\$40{,}000 \text{ (break-even)} = \frac{\$12{,}000}{.30}$$

Graph Showing Break-Even Point

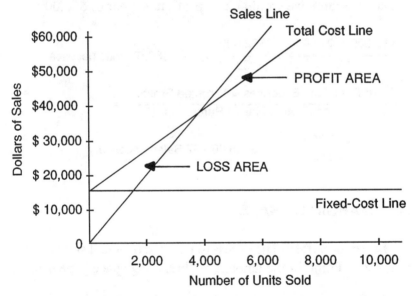

At the sales price of $10 per unit, the more units sold, the more dollars of sales received.

The **Total Cost Line** starts at the left margin at the $12,000 point, which is the total fixed costs. The **Total Cost Line** crosses the sales line at the break-even point (in this case, 4,000 units or $40,000 in sales).

34

4.3 TARGET PROFITS

Target Profits–Useful in planning for sales and costs for future years.

Formula for Target Profits:

$$\frac{\text{Fixed Costs and Expenses} + \text{Targeted Profits}}{\text{Contribution Margin per unit}} = \text{Sales in units necessary}$$

Let us assume we would like a profit next year of $50,000

$$\frac{\$12,000 + \$50,000}{\$3} = \frac{\$62,000}{\$3} = 20,666.67 \text{ units necessary}$$

$$\frac{\text{Fixed Costs and Expenses} = \text{Targeted Profits}}{\text{Contribution Margin Percent}} =$$

$$\frac{\$62,000}{30\%} = \$206,666.67 \text{ Sales necessary}$$

4.4 MARGIN OF SAFETY

Margin of Safety–The excess of targeted or actual sales over Break-Even Point, or the amount of "breathing space" one has.

Computation of Margin of Safety in dollars:

$206,666.67	Targeted Sales
−40,000.00	Break-Even Point in dollars
$166,666.67	Margin of Safety in dollars

This means that although we will try to sell next year

35

$206,666.67 worth of merchandise, we can lose $166,667 of sales and still keep our heads above water at the Break-Even Point of $40,000 sales.

Computation of Margin of Safety as a percent: Divide the margin of safety in dollars by the total projected sales:

$$\frac{\$166,666.67}{\$206,666.67} = 80.6456455\%$$

This means that sales could be down a little over 80% of those projected, and we still would not be in the loss area.

4.5   PROFIT MAXIMIZATION

Profit Maximization (actually cost minimization). Hold down costs to increase profits.

If a company can make two products, and the contribution margin of the first product is $5 per unit and the contribution margin of the second product is $6 per unit, and if all other things are the same, it would pay to produce only the second product.

Differences between accountants' ideas of profit maximization and economists' ideas of profit maximization.

a.   In figuring cost and revenue lines on graphs, accountants always tend to use straight lines while economists can use curved lines.

b.   Economists consider opportunity costs (the loss we suffer from investing our money in the factory when we could have made perhaps more money by investing it elsewhere) while accountants don't usually consider these alternatives.

4.6 THE PROFIT EQUATION

The absorption-type income statement

    a. Sales less variable and fixed costs equal gross profit.

    b. Gross profit less variable and fixed expenses equals operating income.

The contribution-margin-type income statement

    a. Sales less variable costs less variable expenses equal contribution margin.

    b. Contribution margin less fixed costs less fixed expenses equals operating income.

4.7 INCOME TAXES

The effect of income taxes on Cost-Volume-Profit Analysis

A business wants to project a certain income **after** income taxes, so the federal income tax rate must be taken into consideration.

Example:

Targeted Sales	500 units @ $3 =	$1,500
Less cost (variable)	500 units @ $1 =	$ 500
Contribution Margin	500 units @ $2	$1,000
Less Fixed Costs (rent)		– 600
Net Income BEFORE Taxes		$ 400
(Presumed income tax rate 30%)		
Less income tax (30% of $400)		– 120
Net income AFTER tax		$ 280

But suppose we want a targeted **After-Tax** net income of $400. Formula: Let X = Number of units to be produced. (Since sales are $3 per unit, we will let $3X$ = Total Sales. Since variable costs are $1 per unit, let $1X$ = total variable costs.)

$$\begin{array}{c} \text{Sales less variable costs} \\ \text{less fixed costs} \end{array} = \frac{\text{Targeted After-Tax Net Income}}{100\% - \text{Tax Rate}}$$

$$3X - 1X - \$600 = \frac{\$400}{100\% - 30\%}$$

$$3X - 1X - \$600 = \frac{\$400}{.7}$$

$$\begin{aligned} 3X - 1X - \$600 &= \$571.43 \\ 3X - 1X &= \$571.43 + 600 \\ 2X &= \$1{,}171.43 \\ X &= 585.715 \text{ units to be sold in order to make an after-tax net income of \$400.} \end{aligned}$$

PROOF

Sales of	585.715 Units @ $3 =	$1,757.145
Less variable costs:	585.715 Units @ $1 =	585.715
Contribution Margin	585.715 Units @ $2 =	$ 1,171.43
Less fixed costs (given)		−600.00
Net Income before taxes		$ 571.43
Less income taxes (30% of $571.43)		−171.43
Net income after taxes		$ 400.00

4.8   FINDING TARGETED SALES DOLLARS

A college is contemplating whether or not to offer a night course and is trying to determine whether such a course would be profitable. How much tuition would be needed to break even? 80% of the students pay \$1,000 each, and the other 20% of the students receive a discount and pay \$800 each. The variable cost is \$240 per student and the fixed cost for the course is \$5,000. What is the Break-Even Point in tuition dollars?

$$\text{Break} - \text{Even Point in Tuition Dollars} = \cfrac{\text{Fixed Cost}}{1 - \left(\cfrac{\text{Variable Cost per student}}{\text{Tuition per student}} \right)} =$$

$$\cfrac{\$5,000}{1 - \left(\cfrac{\$240}{(.8 \times \$1,000) + (.2 \times \$800)} \right)} = \cfrac{\$5,000}{1 - \left(\cfrac{\$240}{\$800 + \$160} \right)} =$$

$$\cfrac{\$5,000}{1 - \left(\cfrac{\$240}{\$960} \right)} = \cfrac{\$5,000}{1 - .25} = \cfrac{\$5,000}{.75} = \$6,666.67$$

So the course will break even if the college receives a total of \$6666.67 from the students in tuition.

4.9 COST-PROFIT-VOLUME ANALYSIS WITH SEMI-FIXED COSTS

Semi-fixed costs have both fixed and variable elements.

Example: Assume a company is thinking about adding a second shift. Now during the day shift they produce 10,000 units at a variable cost of \$20 per unit and sell these for \$30 per unit. Total fixed costs are \$50,000. If we add an evening shift, the total fixed costs will be \$70,000, and we could produce 15,000 units in total (See Table on next page).

If all the added production could be sold, it would pay to put on an evening shift.

39

	Present Day Shift	Proposed Day and Evening Shifts
Volume in Sales	10,000 units	15,000 units
Sales Revenue	10,000 units @ $30 $300,000	15,000 units @ $30 $450,000
Less Variable Costs	10,000 units @ $20 $200,000	15,000 units @ $20 $300,000
Contribution Margin	10,000 units @ $10 $100,000	15,000 units @ $10 $150,000
Less fixed costs	$–50,000	$–70,000
Net Income	$ 50,000	$ 80,000

4.10   MULTI-PRODUCT COST-PROFIT-VOLUME ANALYSIS

If a company produces several products, it will make more by producing the products with the highest contribution margins.

4.11   SENSITIVITY ANALYSIS

Using "What-If" calculations to determine changes in product mix and Break-Even Points.

4.12   PREDATORY PRICING

Cutting prices immensely to run out the competition (illegal).

4.13   IRRELEVANCE OF PAST (SUNK) COSTS

We bought a factory machine for $70,000 which is no longer

usable. $40,000 has been depreciated over the years, so its book value is now $30,000. We can sell it as scrap for $10,000, so the remaining $20,000 is lost or a "past or sunk cost." It is a loss.

4.14 CAPACITY COSTS

Fixed costs such as taxes and straight-line depreciation.

4.15 CURVILINEAR VARIABLE COSTS

These costs vary with volume of activity, but not proportionately (Semi-variable costs).

4.16 LEARNING CURVE

As new employees work longer on a factory job, they become more efficient and can turn out more usable products per hour.

4.17 DISCRETIONARY COSTS

Fixed costs that are not always necessary to production, in the short run, such as research and advertising.

REVIEW QUESTIONS

1. **How is Contribution Margin computed?**
   Subtract variable costs and expenses from sales.

2. **How is the Contribution Margin ratio computed?**
   Divide contribution margin by sales.

3. **What is the purpose of using Contribution Margin?**
   Financial planning.

4. **How is Break-Even Point in units computed?**

Divide fixed costs and expenses by contribution margin per unit.

5. How is contribution margin per unit computed?
Divide total dollar value of contribution margin by the number of units produced.

6. How is the Break-Even Point in dollars computed?
Divide fixed costs and expenses by contribution margin ratio – sometimes called contribution margin percent.

7. What is the purpose of computing Break-Even Point?
Financial planning.

8. What is the purpose of computing targeted profits?
Financial planning.

Also, it answers such questions as: How many units must we sell in order to make an annual profit of, say, $100,000?

9. How is Margin of Safety computed?
Subtract break-even dollar sales from budgeted or actual dollar sales.

10. How is Margin of Safety computed as a percent?
Divide the margin of safety in dollars by the budgeted or actual sales in dollars.

11. What is the purpose of computing Margin of Safety?
To discover how far projected sales would have to drop before our company would get into the loss area.

12. How do we achieve profit maximization?
By holding down factory costs.

13. What is the profit equation?

Sales less cost of goods sold less operating expenses equal operating income.

Also, Sales less variable costs and expenses, less fixed costs and expenses equal operating income.

14. How does income tax affect profit planning?

Most businessmen are interested in net income **after** tax, so the income tax rate must be computed or "built into" profit planning.

15. How are targeted sales dollars determined?

By taking into consideration both fixed and variable costs in determining Break-Even Point, and then adding to this the desired operating income.

16. How can there sometimes be two levels of fixed costs?

If a company decides to put on an extra shift, the fixed costs will increase.

17. How does the production of more than one product change company planning?

They must decide how much of one product to make and how much of the other products.

18. What do corporations mean by "sensitivity analysis?"

They use the "what-if" analysis and determine the effect on the product mix of one particular change in production or pricing.

19. Why is predatory pricing illegal?

It is a method of extreme price cutting in an attempt to run competition out of business.

20. Why are past costs irrelevant in production planning?

The money spent on unusable plant and equipment is irretrievably gone and cannot be recovered so should have no effect on future plans.

21. What are curvilinear variable costs?
Semi-variable costs.

22. Why do some firms consider learning curves important?
The quickness with which new employees can be trained in the factory affects future planning.

23. Why are discretionary costs important?
These are costs that can be reduced temporarily to hold down expenses – like advertising and research.

CHAPTER 5

PRODUCT COSTING METHODS

5.1 VARIABLE COSTING vs. FULL ABSORPTION COSTING

Variable Costing–A method of product costing where fixed manufacturing overhead is excluded from inventorial costs and expensed immediately in the period incurred.

Absorption Costing–A method of product costing where fixed manufacturing overhead is included in the inventory.

Absorption Costing is used for external reporting purposes.

5.2 OVERHEAD APPLICATION RATES

Since total overhead costs cannot be computed accurately until the end of the fiscal period, the overhead for each job leaving the factory must be computed from overhead rates. These are usually computed at the beginning of each fiscal year by dividing the budgeted fixed overhead by some denominator value such as budgeted hours, budgeted labor costs, or budgeted machine hours. Some factories use a single blanket rate for the whole factory, and others compute a separate rate for each department.

Example:

$$\frac{\text{Budgeted Factory Overhead}}{\text{Budgeted Labor Costs}} = \frac{\$500,000}{\$750,000} = .667 = 66.7\%$$

Thus, budgeted overhead is 66.7% of budgeted direct labor costs. Let us say that a shipment of finished goods is leaving the factory with Direct Material Costs of $500 and Direct Labor Costs of $600. How much overhead cost should be allotted to this shipment? Multiply the direct labor costs of $600 by the overhead application rate of 66.7% (or 2/3) = $400. Therefore, to compute the actual cost of the goods being shipped out, add actual Direct Material of $500, actual Direct Labor of $600, and applied factory overhead of $400 to get a total cost of $1500.

Example:

$$\frac{\text{Budgeted Factory Overhead}}{\text{Budgeted Direct Labor Hours}} = \frac{\$500,000}{200,000 \text{ hours}} = \$2.50 \text{ per hour}$$

If, in the history of the factory, it is found that direct labor hours rise and fall with production and with factory overhead more evenly than do direct labor hours, the owners might decide to use direct labor hours as a denominator in computing the annual overhead rate. Then, as seen above, it is more understandable to use so much per hour in speaking of the application rate. So, if a shipment of finished goods is leaving the factory, and these goods have been worked on for 30 direct labor hours, we multiply 30 times the $2.50 rate and get $75 as the applied factory overhead for this shipment.

Some firms use machine hours and others could use direct material costs or anything else they wish as denominators in computing overhead application rates.

5.3 ACTUAL, NORMAL, OR STANDARD COSTING

Actual Costing–Some first wait until the end of the fiscal period and compute actual overhead before allocating it to the various finished goods shipments. This is more accurate but forces a wait until after the end of the fiscal period at which time the actual overhead costs can be determined as the bills come in. So in **actual** costing the managers use **actual** material costs, **actual** direct labor costs, and **actual** overhead costs.

Normal Costing–The use of actual material costs, actual direct labor costs, and **applied** factory overhead costs.

Standard Costing–The use of standard materials costs, standard direct labor costs, and standard factory overhead costs. Standard costs are worked out by the company planners in advance and are usually expressed in a per-unit basis.

REVIEW QUESTIONS

1. How does variable costing differ from absorption costing?

In variable costing the fixed overhead costs such as rent, taxes, and straight-line depreciation are expensed immediately – placed in the period's income statement as an expense, and not put in an inventory account. In absorption costing, these amounts are placed into either the Work in Process Inventory or the Finished Goods Inventory – asset accounts – until the period in which the products are sold at which time they enter the income statement as Cost of Goods Sold.

2. Why is absorption costing the only one that can be used for external purposes?

The federal government has not approved variable costing for income tax reporting purposes. Net income amounts differ between the two methods – absorption and variable – and the government wants to be sure to receive its full share of income tax revenue.

3. If variable costing cannot be used for external purposes, why have it at all?

Variable costing has proved important to businessmen in financial planning.

4. Why are overhead application rates computed?

Because the cost of a product is needed at the time the product leaves the factory so that a higher sales price can be set, thus giving a needed gross margin – rather than a gross loss. Since the actual overhead amounts cannot be known accurately until year's end, the applied rate gives management a general idea of the cost of the finished goods leaving the factory.

5. Why do some factories compute a blanket or overall application rate and other factories compute application rates for each department?

It depends on the type of product manufactured and the amount of accuracy that management needs.

6. What are the main denominators (divisors) used by various factories in computing overhead rates at the beginning of each fiscal year?

Direct labor costs, direct labor hours, machine hours, and direct material costs.

7. Why do some firms use actual costing, others normal costing, and still others standard costing?

It depends entirely on the management of the firm and how they want to keep their records for internal control. Actual costing is slower but more accurate. Normal costing is faster but less accurate. Standard costing provides the desired answers even sooner but often entails more complicated planning.

CHAPTER 6

JOB ORDER COSTING

6.1   JOB ORDER vs. PROCESS COSTING

Job-Order Cost Accounting is used by firms manufacturing custom-made products such as printers, engineers, manufacturers of ships and trains, defense contractors, highway and dam contractors.

Process Cost Accounting is used by firms using mass production, like auto firms, clothing firms, oil refineries, chemical firms, and flour grinding firms.

6.2   SOURCE DOCUMENTS OF JOB COSTING

Separate documents must be kept for each job – job cost sheets (Details of materials, labor, and overhead costs for each job).

Other records – raw material orders, raw material vouchers, stores requisitions, work tickets, and clock cards.

6.3   COST FLOWS FOR JOB ORDER COSTING

Purchase of Raw Materials–Debit Stores and credit Accounts Payable.

Use of Direct Materials in Factory–Debit Work in Process and credit Stores.

Use of Direct Labor in Factory–Debit Work in Process and credit Wages Payable.

Application of Overhead to Production–Debit Work in Process and credit Factory Overhead Control.

Receipt of Bills for Overhead Costs–Debit Factory Overhead Control and credit various accounts such as Accounts Payable, Cash, and Accumulated Depreciation.

Flow of Finished Goods from Factory to Finished Goods Warehouse–Debit Finished Goods and credit Work in Process.

Flow of Finished Goods from Finished Goods Warehouse to Trucks and Trains When Sold–Debit Cost of Goods Sold and credit Finished Goods for cost price. Also debit Accounts Receivable or Cash and credit Sales for sales price.

6.4 DIRECT AND INDIRECT MATERIALS

When direct materials leave the stores warehouse for the factory, we debit Work in Process and credit Stores (also called Direct Materials Inventory).

When indirect materials (supplies) leave the stores warehouse for the factory, we debit Factory Overhead Control and credit Stores.

6.5 ACCOUNTING FOR LABOR IN JOB ORDER COST ACCOUNTING

Laborers on factory floor fill out work tickets showing the

number of hours worked on each job during the day. These are added to the job cost sheets by the accountants.

The job cost sheets are a subsidiary ledger to Work in Process.

To record the direct labor, the accountant debits Work in Process and also debits the job in the subsidiary ledger, and then credits wages payable.

To record indirect labor, the accountant debits Factory Overhead Control (also debiting indirect labor in the subsidiary ledger) and credits wages payable.

6.6 ACCOUNTING FOR MANUFACTURING OVERHEAD IN JOB ORDER COST ACCOUNTING

Factor Overhead Control is the controlling account in the General Ledger.

Factor Overhead Control usually has a subsidiary ledger with such accounts as Indirect Material (Supplies), Indirect labor, Depreciation Expense, Factory Rent, Factory Taxes, Factory Utilities.

6.7 TRANSFERS TO FINISHED GOODS IN JOB ORDER COST ACCOUNTING

Job Order Cost Accounting means that goods are produced in batches for special customers.

The factory account in the general ledger, Work in Process, will have a subsidiary ledger for each batch. The accounts will be called Job #1, Job #2, Job #3, etc.

The account in the general ledger called Finished Goods

Inventory will often also have a subsidiary ledger, one account for each type of finished goods in the warehouse, such as: regular brooms, janitor brooms, and whisk brooms.

When finished goods leave the factory, the general ledger accounts will be affected as follows: Finished Goods Inventory will be debited and Work in Process Inventory will be credited. Also the subsidiary accounts will be debited and credited as needed, so that at all times the total of all the subsidiary accounts will equal the balance of the controlling account in the general ledger.

6.8 TRANSFERS TO COST OF GOODS SOLD IN JOB ORDER COST ACCOUNTING

When goods are shipped out of the Finished Goods Warehouse, the Cost of Goods Sold account is debited and the Finished Goods Inventory account is credited for the cost price of the goods sold.

The subsidiary account (such as whisk brooms) in the Finished Goods Subsidiary Ledger is also credited for the cost price.

Cash or Accounts Receivable is debited and Sales is credited for the sales price.

6.9 APPLYING FACTORY OVERHEAD

When goods are ready to be shipped out, the actual number of direct labor hours used is multiplied by the previously determined overhead rate to compute the applied factory overhead in dollars. (Or the direct labor costs of producing the goods going out are multiplied by the previously determined overhead rate to compute the applied factory overhead in dollars.)

If there is no Factory Overhead Applied account, the Work in Process Inventory is debited and the Factory Overhead Control Account is credited for the amount of the applied overhead. This is known as applying overhead to production.

If there is an applied overhead account, then Work in Process Inventory is debited and Applied Factory Overhead is credited for the applied amount. Then a second entry is required for the same amount, debiting Factory Overhead Applied and crediting Factory Overhead Control.

Factory Overhead Control		Factory Overhead Applied	
Actual Costs Incurred	Applied Costs	Applied Costs	Applied Costs
Indirect labor 500.00	(2) 1,800.00	(2) 1,800.00	(1) 1,800.00
Indirect Mat. 300.00			
Depr. Expense 100.00			
Utilities 800.00			
Factory Taxes 300.00			
Total Actual	(3) 200.00		
Overhead 2,000.00			

Entry 1: Debit Work in Process Inventory $1,800 and credit Factory Overhead Applied $1,800. (Actual hours worked 600, times applied overhead rate of $3).

Entry 2: Debit Factory Overhead Applied and credit Factory Overhead Control (to close out the Factory Overhead Applied account).

6.10 TWO WAYS OF CLOSING OUT FACTORY OVERHEAD CONTROL

Factory Overhead Control is a temporary account and must be closed at the end of the fiscal year. If most of the goods produced have been sold, the easiest way is merely to close the balance of the Factory Overhead Control account into Cost of Goods Sold.

The Factory Overhead Control account above is underapplied. That is, the $1,800 on the applied (credit) side is less than the $2,000 total incurred on the debit side, giving the account a debit balance of $200. In this case, in order to close the account we could debit Cost of Goods Sold for $200 and credit Factory Overhead Control for $200.

However, if the Factory Overhead Control was overapplied (that is, if it had a credit balance), it would be necessary to debit Factory Overhead Control in order to close it out. In that case, we would debit Factory Overhead Control and credit Cost of Goods Sold.

Second Method: Proration of the balance of Factory Overhead Control to three accounts: Work in Process Inventory, Finished Goods Inventory, and Cost of Goods Sold.

Let us imagine that much of the inventory is still unsold, and that the balance of the Work in Process Inventory account at the end of the year is $100,000. This is the value of the partially finished products still in the factory at year's end. Let us also imagine that there is an ending Finished Goods Inventory of $200,000, the value of the finished goods in the finished goods warehouse that are still unsold. Let us also imagine that the Cost of Goods Sold account at year's end, before it is closed out, has a total of $300,000.

Work in Process Inv.	Finished Goods Inv.	Cost of Goods Sold
Ending Inventory 100,000	Ending Inventory 200,000	300,000

PRORATION PROCESS

Work in Process Ending Inventory	$100,000	16-2/3%
Finished Goods Ending Inventory	$200,000	33-1/3%
Cost of Goods sold	$300,000	50%
TOTAL	$600,000	100%

Let us assume further that Factory Overhead Control has a debit balance of $200, and we want to prorate this amount among the above three accounts in proportion to their respective balances at the end of the fiscal period. Since Work in Process Ending Inventory is 16-2/3% of the total computed above, 16-2/3% of the $200 balance, or in this case $33.33, would be allocated to Work in Process. Since the Finished Goods Ending Inventory is 33-1/3% of the $200 balance, $66.67 would be allocated to Finished Goods. Since Cost of Goods Sold is half of the above balance, $100 would be allocated there. The proration journal entry would appear as follows:

Work in Process Inventory	33.33	
Finished Goods Inventory	66.67	
Cost of Goods Sold	100.00	
Factory Overhead Control		200.00

After this proration journal entry has been posted, the accounts would appear as follows:

Factory Overhead Control		Work in Process		Finished Goods		Cost of Goods Sold	
2,000.00	1,800.00						
	200.00	100,000		200,000		300,000	
			33		67		100

6.11 COMPUTATION OF SPENDING VARIANCES

Let us imagine that we budget $3 per broom handle in making brooms in the broom factory. However, the price has now gone up to $3.10. During the year, we buy from a vendor 50,000 broom handles. What is the spending variance and how is it computed?

Actual number of broom handles purchased
50,000 x $3.10 actual rate = ... $155,000
Actual number of broom handles purchased
50,000 x $3.00 standard rate = ... −150,000
    Unfavorable Spending Variance .... $ 5,000

During the year we have lost $5,000 because of the price increase. We spent too much. The solution might be to seek a new vendor and perhaps buy cheaper broom handles.

6.12 COMPUTATION OF PRODUCTION VOLUME VARIANCES

Let us imagine that during the month we actually produced 50,000 bars of soap. Our standards are 2 lbs. of raw material for every bar of soap. So we multiply 50,000 bars of soap by 2 lbs. and get a standard use of raw material of 100,000 lbs. This means that we should have placed 100,000 lbs. of raw material into the factory in order to get out the 50,000 bars of soap. However, we actually only put in 95,000 lbs. of raw material.

100,000 lbs. raw material standard (should have)	
x $2 standard rate per lb. = ...	$200,000
95,000 lbs. raw material actual	
x $2 standard rate per lb. = ...	$190,000
Favorable Production Volume Variance	$ 10,000

We have a favorable production volume variance and have saved $10,000 since we did not dump as much raw material in as we should have for the actual number of bars of soap that we produced.

6.13   JOB COST SHEETS

Job Cost Sheets–These are a subsidiary ledger to Work in Process Inventory controlling account in job order cost accounting, and at any time the total of all the job cost sheets must match the total of the Work in Process account in the general ledger.

THE BROWN MANUFACTURING COMPANY		Job. No._____	
For stock _____ Customer _____			
Product _____ Date Started _____ Date Completed _____			

DEPARTMENT A								
Direct Material			Direct Labor			Overhead		
Date	Reference	Amount	Date	Reference	Amount	Date	Reference	Amount
	(Store's Requisiton No.)			(Work Ticket No.)				

Detailed records of direct material, direct labor, and factory overhead are kept on the cost sheets. Holding down costs here can make the difference between profit and loss for the company.

6.14 STORES REQUISITIONS

Stores Requisitions–Papers the factory fills out in order to get raw materials from the raw materials (stores) warehouse.

Job No. ____16____
Dept. ____E____
Debit the Account ____Work in Process____
Authorized by ____MRL____ Date ____5/12____

Description	Quantity	Unit Cost	Amount
RL 42 Hasps	10	$2.00	$20.00

6.15 WORK TICKETS

Work Tickets–Used to charge jobs for direct labor used. These are filled out on the factory floor and sent to the cost accountants.

Employee No. 620	Date 3/18	Job No. 16
Operation polishing	Account Wk. in Proc.	Dept. C
		Pieces
Stop 3:45 P.M.	Rate $10.00	Worked: 20
Start 3:00 P.M.	Amount $7.50	Rejected: 0
		Completed: 20

6.16   CLOCK CARDS

Clock Cards–Used to show amount of time worked each day. Often used in conjunction with time clocks.

Name	James Brown			Employee Number		815
Dept.	C			Week Ending		3/18/88

Date	A.M.		P.M.		Excess Hrs.		Total Hours
	In	Out	In	Out	In	Out	
3/14	7:59	12:01	12:59	5:00			8

Regular Time_____ hrs. @_____ _____
Overtime Premium_____ hrs. @_____ _____
Gross Earnings   _____

6.17   RESPONSIBILITY CENTERS

Responsibility Centers–A specific part of the organization assigned to a manager who is then held accountable for its operation and resources.

Example: Jean Brown starts a Swedish Restaurant. Later, after a successful start, she decides to expand and also have a catering service. She hires Chuck Smith to run the catering service and hires Mary Brown to run the restaurant section. Each of these people is responsible for his/her own part of the business, including controlling costs and revenues. Jean Brown still has control over the entire operation – doing such things a paying the rent and handling the overall bookkeeping records.

REVIEW QUESTIONS

1. How does job order cost accounting differ from process cost accounting?

Job order is set up for firms manufacturing "made to order" or custom-made products, while process costing is for mass production firms.

2. What are job cost sheets?

Cards with details of each job going through the factory, including costs of direct material, direct labor, and factory overhead.

3. What are other source documents besides job cost sheets?

Clock cards, raw material vouchers, stores requisitions, and work tickets.

4. How do costs flow through a factory using job order cost accounting?

Raw materials are purchased and then stored in a raw materials warehouse. Then these are used in the factory. The finished goods leave the factory and are stored in the finished goods warehouse until sold.

5. How do direct materials differ from indirect materials?

Direct materials are used directly on the goods being manufactured, such as wood used in broom handles. Indirect materials are supplies like janitor cleaning compound that are not used directly in making the brooms.

6. How are direct materials accounted for differently from indirect materials?

When direct materials leave the storehouse to be used in the factory, Work in Process Inventory is debited and Stores is credited. On the other hand, when indirect materials (supplies) leave the storehouse to be used in the factory, Factory Overhead Control is debited and Stores account is credited.

7. Where are the Job Cost Sheets kept?

Job Cost Sheets are a subsidiary to Work in Process Inventory and are a part of the factory accounting.

8. How does direct labor differ from indirect labor?

Direct laborers work directly on the factory production line. Indirect laborers do not. Examples of indirect laborers would be factory janitors and factory superintendents.

9. How does accounting differ between direct labor costs and indirect labor costs?

To charge direct labor to production, we debit Work in Process and credit Wages Payable. To charge indirect labor we debit Factory Overhead Control and credit Wages Payable.

10. What accounts might be found in a subsidiary ledger of the Manufacturing Overhead Control account?

Factory Rent, Factory Utilities, Depreciation Expense for Factory Machinery, Factory Taxes.

11. What is the accounting procedure when finished products leave the factory?

Debit Finished Goods Inventory and credit Work in Process Inventory.

12. What entries are made on the books when goods are sold?

Debit Cost of Goods Sold and credit Finished Goods Inventory for the cost price of the goods, and also debit either Cash or Accounts Receivable and credit Sales for the sales price of the goods.

13. How do you apply overhead to production if the firm has no Factory Overhead Applied account?

Debit Work in Process Inventory and credit Factory Overhead Control.

14. Why do some firms use a Factory Overhead Applied account and other firms do not?

The firms using a Factory Overhead Applied account think that it is theoretically more sound because the applied amount is just a guess and not the actual amount.

15. How do you apply overhead to production if the firm does have a Factory Overhead Applied account?

Debit Work in Process Inventory and credit Factory Overhead Applied.

16. How do we close out the Factory Overhead Applied account?

Debit Factory Overhead Applied and credit Factory Overhead Control.

17. How do we close out the Factory Overhead Control account?

Most firms close it out into Cost of Goods Sold. Other firms close it out into three accounts: Work in Process Inventory, Finished Goods Inventory, and Cost of Goods Sold, by prorating the balance of the Factory Overhead Control account proportionally to the respective balances of Work in Process Inventory, Finished Goods Inventory, and Cost of Goods Sold, at the end of the fiscal period.

18. What is meant when one states that factory overhead is overapplied?

The credit side of the Factory Overhead Control account is larger than the debit side. We guessed that the overhead expenses would be higher than they actually were.

19. What is meant when one states that factory overhead is underapplied?

The credit side of the Factory Overhead Control account is smaller than the debit side. We guessed that the overhead expenses would be lower than they actually were.

20. Is overapplied factory overhead favorable or unfavorable?

It is favorable, because actual expenses were lower than we thought they would be.

CHAPTER 7

PROCESS COSTING

7.1 WHAT PROCESS COSTING DOES

Process Costing–It assigns the manufacturing costs incurred in each department to the units that have been produced in that department.

7.2 EQUIVALENT UNITS

Equivalent Units–the number of units of work actually done by a producing department in one month.

7.3 ASSIGNING COSTS TO UNITS

Assigning Costs to Units–If Dept. A had $6,000 in costs during the month and produced 600 units, divide 600 units into $6,000 and get a unit cost of $10 per unit.

7.4 INCOMPLETE UNITS IN BEGINNING AND ENDING INVENTORIES (FIRST-IN, FIRST-OUT)

DEPT. A

Beginning Inv.
12 units
2/3 completed
last month

In this month:
63 units

Total 75 units
to account for

Out:
60 units

Ending Inventory
15 units 1/3
completed

The equivalent units are used as a divisor in determining unit costs. Thus, if total costs of the Department A were $10,000, we divide $10,000 by 57 equivalent units to get approximately $175.44 cost per unit.

Total Units Going Through Dept. A

Quantity Schedule

Beginning Inventory ..... 12 units
Plus units coming in
   during month .... 63 units
Total units available ..... 75 units
Less units going out ..... 60 units
Units still left in the
   Ending Inventory .... 15 units

Computation of Equivalent Work Units:

No. of Units needed
to complete beginning
inventory—1/3 of 12 ...... 4 equiv.
units

No. of units both begun
and completed this
month (60–12)............ 48 units
No of work units in ending
inventory—1/3 x 15 ...... 5 equiv.
units

Total Equivalent units
(work units) done by
Dept. A this month .... 57 equiv.
units

7.5 PRODUCTION COST REPORT

Production Cost Report–This adds dollar values in addition to unit computations:

PRODUCTION REPORT

Cost to be accounted for:	
Work in process, beginning	$ 5,103.20
Cost added by the department	
(63 units @ $100)	$ 6,300.00
Total Cost to be accounted for	$11,403.20
Work in Process, Ending	
(5 units @ $175.44)	$ 877.20
Transferred to next department	
(60 units @ $175.44)	$10,526.00

7.6 SPOILAGE COMPUTATIONS

Normal Spoilage–What happens under efficient operating conditions – It is an inherent result of the manufacturing process.

Abnormal Spoilage–Not expected under proper operating conditions.

Normal Spoilage is planned spoilage and is a cost of doing business. It should be debited to Cost of Goods Sold.

Abnormal Spoilage should be expensed immediately.

Examples:

    a. Writing off normal spoilage costs:

           Cost of Goods Sold   500

               Work in Process   500

b. Writing off abnormal spoilage costs:
Loss from Abnormal Spoilage   500
Work in Process   500

7.7   SEQUENTIAL PROCESSING

Sequential Processing–Goods going through the factory in logical order – that is, Dept. A, then Dept. B, then Dept. C.

7.8   PARALLEL PROCESSING

Parallel Processing–Goods going through the factory in some order other than Sequential. In making different products, some goods might go through Dept. A, then Dept. B, then Dept. C. Other goods might go through Dept. A, then Dept. D, then Dept. E.

7.9   FLOW OF MATERIALS, LABOR AND OVER-HEAD COSTS IN PROCESS COSTING

Raw Materials Warehouse, Dept. I of Factory, Dept. II of Factory, Dept. III of Factory, Dept. IV of Factory, Finished Goods Warehouse, then sold.

REVIEW QUESTIONS

1. How does Process Costing differ from Job Order Costing?
It figures equivalent cost per unit.

2. What are equivalent units?
Work units in the department for one month.

3. How is a Quantity Schedule developed?
Add actual units in the beginning inventory and actual units

coming in during the month and deduct units going out, to get units left in ending inventory.

4. How are equivalent units computed?

Add the number of work units needed to complete the beginning inventory and the number of units both begun and completed this month, and the number of work units in the ending inventory.

5. What is the value of the Production Report?

It shows both in units and in dollars what happened in the production department during the month.

6. How does accounting for normal spoilage differ from accounting for abnormal spoilage?

A cost account is debited for normal spoilage and an expense account is debited for abnormal spoilage.

7. How does Sequential Processing of materials in a factory differ from Parallel Processing?

Sequential processing goes in 1-2-3 order – that is, from Dept. 1 to Dept. 2 to Dept. 3, etc. Parallel Processing goes in some other order depending on what products are made. For instance, one product might travel through Dept. 1, then Dept. 4, then Dept 5. Another might travel through Dept. 1, then 2, then 3.

8. How does the flow of materials in Process Cost Accounting differ from the flow of materials in Job Order Cost Accounting?

There are no separate batches or jobs in Process Cost. Also there are likely to be several departments in the factory through which costs flow.

CHAPTER 8

COST ALLOCATION IN SERVICE DEPARTMENTS AND SEGMENTED REPORTING

8.1 THE NATURE OF SERVICE DEPARTMENTS

Service departments are support centers, such as a hospital laundry or a hospital cafeteria. Costs of these service departments build up and must be allocated to the various producing departments which then in turn must be allocated to the various products manufactured.

Allocation bases–Hours worked, kilowatt hours of electricity used, proportional amount of floor space, proportional amount of payroll dollars.

8.2 DIRECT METHOD OF ALLOCATION OF COSTS

The direct costs of departments are first accumulated in service department accounts. Then the service department accounts are allocated directly to user departments without going through intermediate departments. There are no cost allocations between service departments in this method.

8.3 THE STEP METHOD OF ALLOCATION OF COSTS

The direct costs of departments are first accumulated in the service department accounts. The allocations usually begin with closing the account of the service department that services the greatest number of other departments. Once an allocation is made from a service department, no further allocations are made back to that department. Each service department in turn is closed out into the other remaining service departments and into the production departments, until finally all the service department accounts are closed out.

8.4   THE RECIPROCAL METHOD

The direct costs of departments are first accumulated in the service department accounts. Accounts are closed out into each other simultaneously using matrix algebra, accounting for cost flows in both directions among service departments that provide services to one another. At the end of this, all service department accounts are closed out into production department accounts.

8.5   PLANTWIDE vs. DEPARTMENT RATES

Once service department costs have been allocated to production departments, the total production department costs must then be allocated to the various jobs going through the factory. This is done by using labor rates or machine-hour rates. If all departments are similar (that is, all labor-intensive, or perhaps all machine-intensive), they might use plantwide rates. But if some departments are machine-intensive and other departments labor-intensive, it would be better to use departmental rates – with the labor-intensive departments using labor hours and machine-intensive departments using machine hours as rates in the cost allocation.

8.6   ENGINEERED COSTS, DISCRETIONARY
COSTS, AND COMMITTED COSTS

Engineered Costs–Result from a relationship between

inputs and outputs (direct labor costs, direct material costs).

Discretionary Costs–Costs arising from management decisions with no specific relationship to inputs (advertising, health care, research).

Committed Costs–Long-term purchases like land and buildings from which returns can be had only in the far future.

8.7   OPERATING LEVERAGE

Operating Leverage–The ability of a manager to increase his profits a great deal percentagewise with only a small increase percentagewise in sales. This leverage figure is found by dividing contribution margin by net income.

Example: Company A

$$\frac{\text{Contribution Margin } \$40,000}{\text{Net Income } \$10,000} = 4 \text{ operating leverage}$$

Thus, if we increase sales by 10%, we will increase net income by 40%.

	Income Statement Before		Income Statement After
Sales	$100,000	+10% increase	$110,000
Less 60% var. costs	− 60,000		66,000
ContributionMargin	$ 40,000		$ 44,000
Less fixed costs	−30,000		−30,000
Net income	$10,000	+40% increase	$ 14,000

71

REVIEW QUESTIONS

1. How do service departments of a factory differ from producing departments?

Both build up expenses, but only the producing departments make money. So service department expenses must be allocated to producing departments.

2. Give examples of service departments and producing departments.

Producing Departments could be grinding, polishing, and finishing. Service Departments could be training, cafeteria, repair.

3. How can service department costs be fairly allocated to producing departments?

A base must be found as to how the producing department uses the service department. For instance, a repair department might use as an allocation base the number of hours the repairmen work on the producing department's machines.

4. How does the Direct Method of cost allocation differ from the Step Method?

If all the service departments' costs are closed out directly into the accounts of the producing departments, then this is the direct method. On the other hand, if one service department's costs are closed out into the other service departments and also into the producing departments, this is the step method of cost allocation.

5. How does one explain the Reciprocal Method of cost allocation?

Sometimes one service department – Dept. A, uses the services of another service department – Dept. B, while Dept. B also uses Dept. A. Let us say that the Repair Department workers eat at the Company Cafeteria, but the Repair Department workers also fix the stoves and sinks and dishwashing machines of the cafeteria. Then the Reciprocal Method of allocation comes into play. A matrix algebra formula is used to allocate all departments at the same time. This method, in these circumstances, is more complex but more accurate.

6. Should a firm use plantwide rates or departmental rates in allocating costs from service departments to production departments?

This depends on whether the various departments are all fairly labor-intensive or all fairly machine-intensive. If all are fairly similar in these respects, a plantwide rate might be satisfactory. If not, then use separate departmental rates in order to get more accurate allocations.

7. Why is Operating Leverage important?

It is one of the tools management can use for future financial and industrial planning. In certain situations management can use more assets or sales to bring in a much higher percentage return in net profits.

CHAPTER 9

VARIABLE COSTING

9.1 DIFFERENCE BETWEEN VARIABLE AND FULL (ABSORPTION) COSTING

In variable costing the fixed factory overhead costs are placed as expenses in the income statement of the month incurred, while in full absorption costing these costs become part of inventory and are only expensed in the month sold.

Effect of variable costing on profits.

a. As long as in any one month the units sold equal the units produced, the net income will be the same for either method.

b. If **more** units are produced than sold in any one month, the net income under the variable costing method will be less than the net income under the absorption method.

Example: Suppose that fixed factory overhead incurred the first month was $1,800. Also suppose that 3,000 units were produced that month but only 2,900 units were sold. Assume that the planned number of units to be produced was 3,000 units. Divide $1,800 by 3,000 units = $.60 fixed overhead rate per unit.

Fixed Factory Overhead to Account for	Variable Costing– Inventoried Costs	Expense This Year
	(expires immediately as a period cost.)	
$1,800		$1,800

Fixed Factory Overhead to Account for	Absorption Costing– Inventoried Costs	Expense This Year
$1,800	Additions to inventory: 3,000 x $.60 = $1,800	
	Cost of Goods Sold: 2,900 x $.60 = $1,740	$1,740
	Ending Inventory 100 x $.60 = $ 60	

c. If fewer units are produced than sold in any one month, the net income under the variable costing method will be more than the net income under the absorption method.

9.2 ADVANTAGES OF VARIABLE COSTING

Useful only for internal purposes within a company.

    a. Measurement of performance achievement.

    b. Measurement of cost analysis.

Useful in deciding whether or not to accept a one-time sales contract at a lower price.

Useful in deciding whether to make or buy a product.

9.3 ADVANTAGES OF ABSORPTION COSTING

Recognized by the Internal Revenue Service.

Recognized by the public accounting profession.

Used more widely than is variable costing.

REVIEW QUESTIONS

1. Which method is older, absorption or variable costing?
Absorption.

2. Can both absorption and variable costing be used legally for external reporting?
No. So far, only absorption costing can be used externally.

3. What is another name for absorption costing?
Full costing.

4. What is another name for variable costing?
Direct costing.

5. Why is variable costing becoming increasingly popular?
For internal planning.

6. What is the effect of variable costing on profits, as compared with absorption costing?
If production equals sales, there is no difference in profits. If production is greater than sales, net income will be less under the variable costing method than under the absorption costing method. If production is less than sales, the net income will be greater under the variable costing method.

7. Why does the government not allow variable costing procedures for income tax purposes?

Since profits are not the same between the two methods, the government fears it will not receive enough tax revenue if the variable costing methods were allowed.

CHAPTER 10

MASTER BUDGETS AND STANDARDS

10.1 PURPOSE OF BUDGETS

To set financial plans for the future.

10.2 TIME COVERAGE OF BUDGETS

The usual budget is for one year in the future. However some budgets go for three years, five years, and even ten years. The further into the future these plans go, the less accurate they are.

10.3 PRO FORMA STATEMENTS

Income Statements, Balance Sheets, and other financial statements geared for future months and/or years.

10.4 OPERATION BUDGET

A combination of all the subsidiary budgets including sales budget, production budget, material, labor and overhead budgets, cost budget, expense budget, budgeted income statement, capital budget, cash budget, budgeted balance sheet, and budgeted statement of changes in financial position.

10.5 FINANCIAL BUDGET

The last section of subsidiary budgets including capital budget, cash budget, budgeted balance sheet, and budgeted statement of changes in financial position.

10.6 SALES BUDGET

cornerstone

The first budget worked on. Projected future sales must be known before any of the other budgets can be completed.

Example:

SALES BUDGET

	Units	Selling Price	Total Sales
Product A	8,000	$5 per unit	$ 40,000
Product B	20,000	$6 per unit	$120,000
TOTAL............................			$160,000

10.7 PRODUCTION BUDGET

Once the Sales Budget is made, then the Production Budget can be made by adding the Budgeted Sales as computed in the Sales budget to the targeted ending finished goods inventory and deducting from this the beginning finished goods inventory.

PRODUCTION BUDGET IN UNITS

	Product A	Product B
Budgeted Sales (From Sales Budget)	8,000	20,000
Plus Targeted Ending Inventory	10,000	15,000
Total...	18,000	35,000
Less Beginning Finished Goods Inventory .	3,000	5,000
Units to be Produced	15,000	30,000

79

10.8 DIRECT LABOR BUDGET

Once the planned production for the next year is known, a Direct Labor Budget can be calculated.

Example:

DIRECT LABOR BUDGET

	Units of Production	Direct Labor Hrs. Per Unit	Total Hours	Rate Per Hr.	Total Budget
Product A	15,000	3	45,000	$10.00	$ 450,000
Product B	30,000	5	150,000	10.00	1,500,000
Total			195,000		$1,950,000

10.9 COST OF GOODS SOLD BUDGET

Example:

COST OF GOODS SOLD BUDGET

Beginning Finished Goods Inventory:		
Product A: 3,000 units @ $10 =	$ 30,000	
Product B: 5,000 units @ $12 =	$ 60,000	$ 90,000
Plus Cost of Goods Manufactured *(WIP Invty)*		$500,000
Cost of Goods Available for Sale		$590,000
Less Ending Finished Goods Inventory:		
Product A: 10,000 units @ $10 =	$100,000	
Product B: 15,000 units @ $12 =	$180,000	−$280,000
Cost of Goods Sold		$310,000

10.10 CASH BUDGET

One of the last budgets to be made is the Cash Budget, because a great deal of information must be compiled before there are enough figures gathered together to form a Cash Budget. The main purpose of this is to forecast future cash flow in order to determine whether or not money needs to be borrowed or (if there is too much cash) invested at certain times in the following year.

CASH BUDGET JANUARY

Beginning Cash Balance	$12,000
Plus Collections from Customers	$ 3,000
Total cash available	$15,000
Less Probable Disbursements	$14,000
Difference	$ 1,000
Minimum Cash Balance Desired	$ 5,000
Additional Cash Needed	$ 4,000
Borrowings	$ 4,000
Cash Balance – End of Month	$ 5,000

10.11 PARTICIPATIVE BUDGETING

Each department head should sit in on committee meetings and help plan the budget. In this way the department heads will feel they have had input into the budgeting process and will feel that the budgets have not been forced upon them entirely by the higher administrative levels of the corporation.

10.12 THE DELPHI TECHNIQUE (To help forecasting and reduce bias)

Members of the Budget Committee, after discussing the budget with one another, prepare individual budgets and submit them into a basket without placing their names on the budgets that they have prepared. Each group member gets copies of all forecasts. The group discusses the results. Differences between individual forecasts can be discussed without personality bias. Then each group submits another forecast, with discussions as before. The process is continued until a single budget for the following year is agreed upon.

REVIEW QUESTIONS

1. Why are budgets so important in modern-day business?
They are financial plans for the future. They get department heads to plan together and work together more harmoniously, and at year's end they allow comparisons between budgeted and actual items in order to get variances.

2. What is a Pro Forma Income Statement?
An income statement planned for a future year.

3. What is an Operation Budget?
A combination of all the subsidiary budgets of a corporation into one combined budget.

4. What is a Financial Budget?
A combination of capital budget, cash budget, budgeted balance sheet, and budgeted statement of changes in financial position.

5. Why is a Sales Budget the first one planned?
Without sales, there is no need for production.

6. Why is the Cash Budget one of the last budgets made?
Much other information must first be known before the Cash Budget can be prepared.

7. What is the purpose of the Cash Budget?

To show cash flow for each month or quarter of the following year with the idea of finding times of the year when there is either too much cash on hand or too little cash on hand. If there are times with too much cash, short-term investment decisions should be considered. If there are times with too little cash, various means of borrowing money on a short-term basis must be looked into.

8. Why is Participative Budgeting important?

Too many people think budgets are forced upon them and they secretly fight them. They need to be made to feel that they are part of the budgeting process.

9. Why is the Delphi Technique considered?

It is an anonymous method of bringing together ideas of many leading people in the company without getting personalities into the decisions.

CHAPTER 11

FLEXIBLE BUDGETS

11.1 FLEXIBLE BUDGETS

Flexible Budgets–Really several budgets at various levels of production.

At year's end we can compare actual results with the budget that most nearly conforms to the units actually produced in that year, to get variances.

Example:

	Per Unit	Flexible Budget or Master Budget			
Sales in Units		10,000	20,000	30,000	40,000
Sales in dollars....$5		$50,000	$100,000	$150,000	$200,000
Direct Materials ...$2		20,000	40,000	60,000	80,000

The item we make, say brooms, sells for $5 each, so if we make 10,000 brooms next year, the sales in dollars will be $50,000. If we make 20,000 brooms next year, the sales in dollars will be $100,000, and so on.

The direct materials going into the brooms are a variable cost of $2 per broom. So if we manufacture and sell 10,000 brooms next year, the cost will be $20,000. If we manufacture and sell 20,000 brooms next year, the cost will be $40,000, and so on.

At the end of the year we have manufactured and sold 30,000 brooms, so we compare the actual results with the budget for 30,000 brooms as follows:

Comparison of Actual Use and Flexible Budget

Budgeted sales in units... 30,000 units
Actual sales in units .... 30,000 units

	Actual Sales 30,000 units	Budget Based on 30,000 units	Variances
Sales	$160,000	$150,000	$10,000 Favorable
Direct Materials	63,000	60,000	3,000 Unfavorable

Since 30,000 units were actually produced and sold, only the 30,000 unit flexible budget is used for comparison. The actual sales and costs are listed in the first column, and the 30,000 unit budget figures are placed in the second column. Then the two are subtracted.

The sales of brooms of 30,000 units @ $5 were budgeted to bring in $150,000, but evidently the price of the brooms must have increased, since the sales revenues for the year were actually $160,000. The variance (difference) of $10,000 was favorable to the company because the sales were $10,000 higher than predicted for that level of activity.

Direct material costs were budgeted at $2 per unit. Multiplying this by 30,000 units we get a budgeted direct material cost of

$60,000. However the actual direct material costs for the year came to $63,000. Subtracting $60,000 from $63,000 we get an unfavorable direct materials variance because we spent $3,000 more than anticipated. Management is especially interested in the causes of large unfavorable variances and will probably look into this to discover the reasons for this cost overrun.

11.2 CONTINUOUS (Perpetual) BUDGETS

Continuous (Perpetual) Budgets–Cover a year but constantly add a new month on the end as the current month is completed. It keeps management thinking and planning a full twelve months ahead. It keeps management looking twelve months ahead rather than lesser periods.

11.3 PARTICIPATIVE (Self Imposed) BUDGETS

Individual department managers are allowed to prepare their own preliminary budgets. (If a budget is imposed upon a manager from above, it may generate resentment and ill will rather than cooperation and increased productivity.)

Employees in the organization are looked upon as members of a team and all important contributors to the work of the factory.

A person will probably be more apt to work at and work with a budget that he has been a part of producing, than with one imposed on him from above.

If people making their own budget cannot meet the budget requirements, they have only themselves to blame.

11.4 SALES FORECASTING

Sales Forecasting–A sales forecast is usually prepared

before making a sales budget. It is often broader than a sales budget and might include the entire industry.

Some of the factors in making a sales forecast might include sales volumes in past years, pricing policy, unfilled order backlogs, market research, general economic conditions and conditions within our industry, advertising, industry competition, and our share of the market.

Using all the above information, especially sales results in the immediate past, and talking with salesmen in the field, sales projections for next year can be made.

Finally, a sales budget is made from the sales forecast material.

11.5 JUST-IN-TIME INVENTORY SYSTEMS

Just-In-Time Inventory Systems—Using smaller ending Raw Materials Inventories and Finished Goods Inventories.

Popular in recent years.

Made feasible by quick information on inventories now provided by computers.

Made feasible by faster shipping methods and more reliable suppliers.

Cheaper for factories to keep smaller inventories on hand.

Elements for a successful Just-in-Time Inventory System:

a. Company should rely on a few suppliers with long-term contracts.

b. Suppliers must be willing and able to make frequent deliveries in small lots – even as many as several times a day.

c. A company must develop **Total Quality Control** over parts and materials. No defects can be allowed. There must be **Continuous Monitoring** of all materials.

11.6 ZERO-BASE BUDGETING (In-Depth Review)

Used mainly in government and service-type organizations.

Managers are required to start at zero budget levels every year and justify all costs as if programs involved were being started for the first time.

No costs are considered ongoing in nature.

Each year the department manager must rank **all activities in the department according to relative importance.**

Management can then evaluate each decision package independently and pare back in those areas that appear less critical or in those activities with costs too expensive.

In most other budgeting, managers start with last year's budget and simply add to it or subtract from it.

REVIEW QUESTIONS

1. How do flexible budgets differ from static budgets?
Static budget is merely one budget from which we compare actual results at year's end. On the other hand, flexible budgets are a series of budgets at various anticipated production levels.

2. What is another name for flexible budget?
Master budget.

3. How are variances determined?
For each revenue, cost, or expense category in the budgeted income statement, subtract the actual amount from the budgeted amount to get either a favorable or an unfavorable variance.

4. What is the purpose of determining variances in each category?
Management might want to look further into the larger variances to determine the causes of these with the idea of trying to eliminate these large variances in future years.

5. Why are flexible budgets usually preferred over static budgets?
At year's end, only the flexible budget nearest in production to the actual amount produced is used to subtract and determine variances.

6. Why do some managers like Perpetual Budgets?
They roll over every month adding a new month one year ahead to the budget and dropping a month. They force management to look continually a year ahead rather than looking only a shorter period of time into the future.

7. How does sales forecasting differ from sales budgeting?
Sales forecasting is done first, and usually consists of gathering information over a wide range, perhaps from the economy and the industry as a whole, through research and interviews. Then this is condensed into a sales budget for the firm itself.